DIRIGIBLE

DIRIGIBLE

written and illustrated by
Joshua Stoff

Atheneum   **1985**   New York

Library of Congress Cataloging-in-Publication Data

Stoff, Joshua.   Dirigible.

SUMMARY: Describes the building, launching, missions,
and final dismantling of a hypothetical rigid airship,
based on the careers of two Navy dirigibles.
1. Airships—Juvenile literature.   [1. Airships]
I. Title.
TL650.S86 1985   629.133'24   85-7461
ISBN 0-689-31084-6

Published simultaneously in Canada by
Collier Macmillan Canada, Inc.
Type set by Linoprint Composition, New York City
Printed and bound by Maple-Vail, Binghamton, New York
Layouts by Benjamin Birnbaum
First Edition

*To all of those who built
and flew rigid airships*

*and to those of us
who still believe
in the dream.*

DIRIGIBLE

Rigid airships (dirigibles) are no longer "Queens of the Skies." But, fifty years ago, dirigibles flew passengers swiftly and safely to the far corners of the world. Others were used by the Navy as long-range scouts in the days when airplanes could not fly very far. In their day, dirigibles were the pride of their nations, and they are still the largest vehicles that ever flew. A great deal of time, effort and hope went into their design and construction but, because of accidents and some bad management decisions, they no longer exist.

The airship depicted in this tale, the *Long Island,* is not real, but it is an accurate portrayal of the U.S.S. *Los Angeles* (built 1924—ordered dismantled 1940) and it combines many of the operations of this and two other U.S. Navy airships: the *Akron* and *Macon* (1930-1935). There were airship bases, in reality, at Lakehurst, New Jersey in the East and at Moffet Field, California, in the West. The hangars and mooring masts depicted are accurate renderings of those that existed at these two fields. The airship tender described was the U.S.S. *Patoka.*

During the early days of aviation, in 1923 to be exact, several leaders in the United States Naval Air Service decided that they wanted to have a newer and better airship, the kind known as a dirigible, for their fleet. This rigid airship would be a huge flying machine seven hundred feet long, able to carry seventy-five crewmen! It would be able to fly farther and for a longer time without landing than any airplanes of the day. The Navy planned to use dirigibles for long-range scouting.

This type of airship was called "rigid" because, unlike blimps and balloons, it was built upon an aluminum framework to give it its shape. The design was based upon the ideas of the great German airship builder, Count Von Zeppelin, who started constructing them in 1900.

The Navy decided to build the new dirigible at their airship base at Freehold, Long Island. Long Island, located just east of New York City, was an excellent place for an airship base because the land was flat, near to the sea, and was close to railroad lines. Needed materials could easily be brought in. A huge hangar, which had once housed other airships, was already there. Construction could begin soon.

A dirigible is a lighter-than-air craft that can be steered. Airships were lighter-than-air because they were filled with the safe gas, helium. Helium is lighter than the surrounding air and an airship filled with this gas rises easily. The engines, which are attached to the sides of the airship, have propellers mounted on them to provide thrust, allowing the dirigible to move forward.

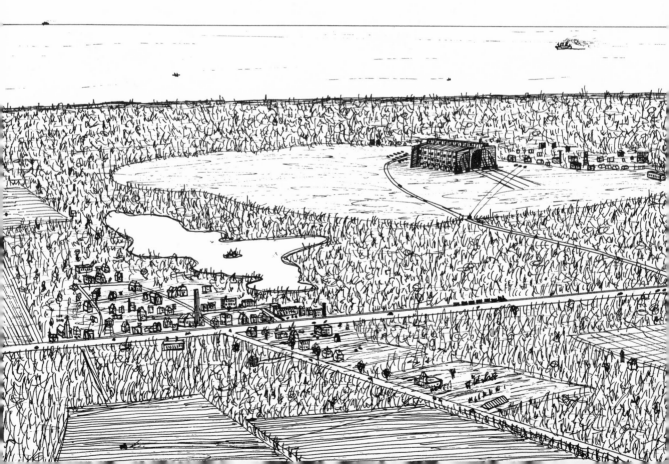

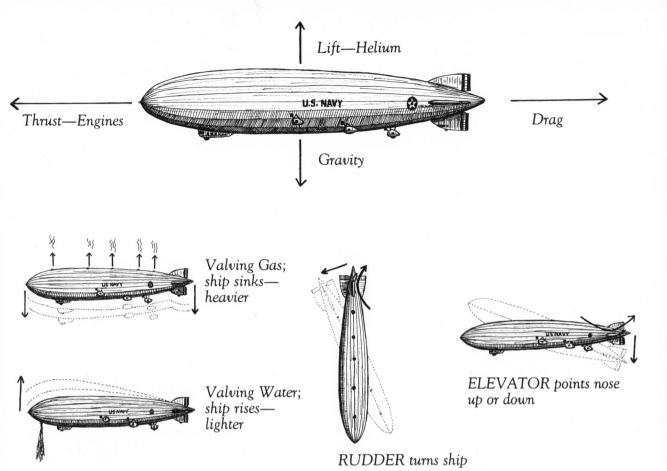

Lift—Helium

Thrust—Engines

U.S. NAVY

Drag

Gravity

Valving Gas;
ship sinks—
heavier

Valving Water;
ship rises—
lighter

RUDDER *turns ship*

ELEVATOR *points nose
up or down*

The force of the air passing over the airship causes resistance (drag), just as it does on airplanes. Because of this, airships were streamlined. They were long and skinny with a pointed nose and fins. Streamlining created less drag, and allowed an airship to move faster through the air. One could fly 80 miles an hour!

The dirigible contained gas cells filled with helium. If the airship wanted to descend it released some helium, making it heavier, and it would go down slowly. Airships also carried water ballast that could be dumped to make the airship lighter so that it would rise. Rudders on the fins could be turned sideways to steer it. Elevators in the tail could be moved up or down to point the airship's nose up or down.

7

Rigid airships had solid aluminum frameworks that gave them their shape. The framework was covered with a fabric to protect everything inside. Within the framework there were ten separate gas cells filled with helium. The gas cells were held in place by a wire netting. There were walkways through the entire airship, as well as many interior rooms and storage areas. Engine gondolas were attached to the outside. All operations of the ship were controlled from the control car, located on the bottom. It was here that the captain was stationed. This new dirigible would be equipped to carry five biplane (double winged) fighters—to be used as long-range scouts. They could be launched and recovered in flight. This made the airship a flying aircraft carrier.

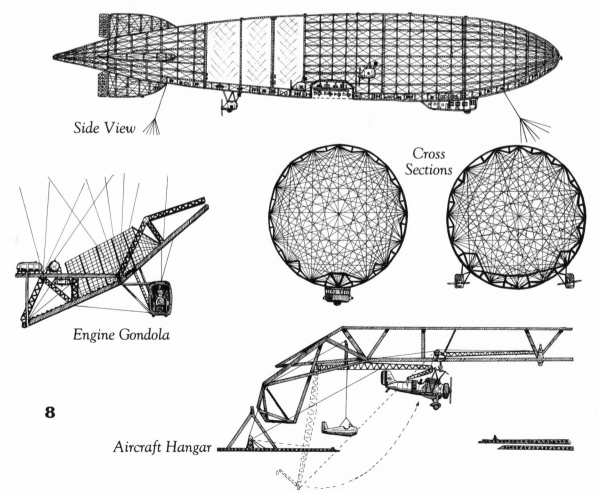

Side View

Cross Sections

Engine Gondola

Aircraft Hangar

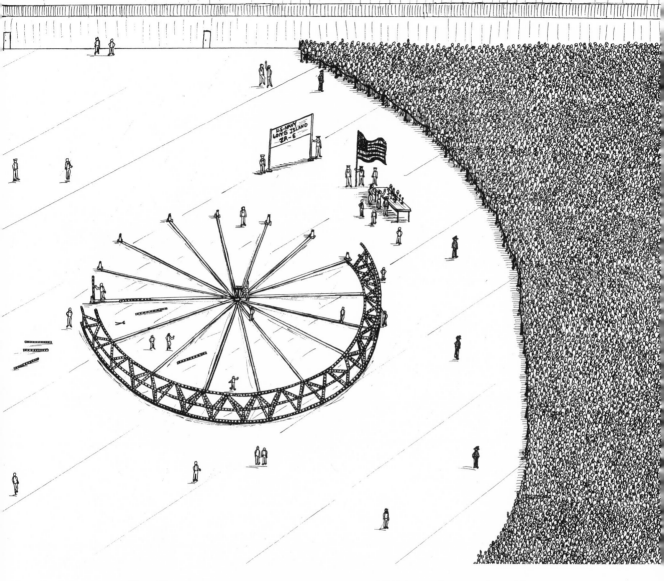

Finally, on a sunny morning in 1924, a huge crowd attended a ceremony celebrating the beginning of construction of this new dirigible. Important people gave speeches describing the wonders of this future airship.

Construction began first on the main rings of the dirigible. Aluminum was used because it was very strong and light. Small girders were riveted together and assembled into the main rings. Special riveting tools were developed for this job.

9

These rings had several strong main joints where the girders were attached to each other. The girders were made with holes in them so that they would be as light as possible.

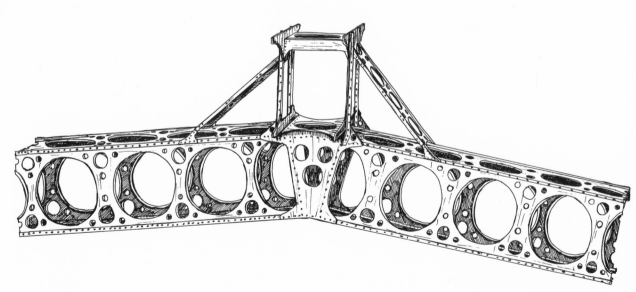

In all, about two hundred men were required to assemble
the airship frame.

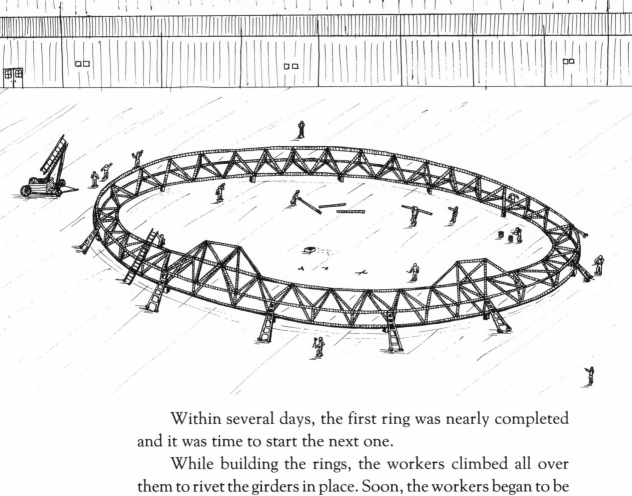

Within several days, the first ring was nearly completed and it was time to start the next one.

While building the rings, the workers climbed all over them to rivet the girders in place. Soon, the workers began to be dwarfed by the size of the airship.

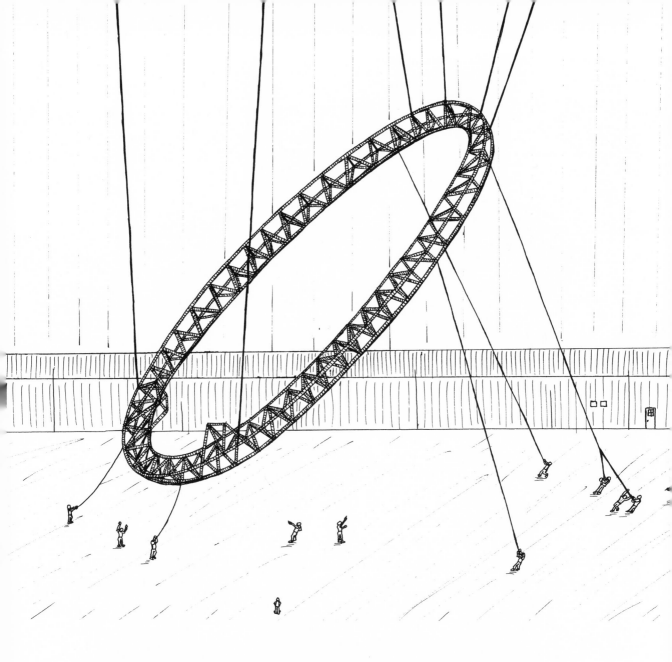

When they were finished, the main rings were hauled up
to the ceiling with pulleys and hung in position vertically.
Workers pulled ropes attached to the bottoms of the rings to
direct them into the proper place. They were so big that they
nearly filled the space between the floor and ceiling.

13

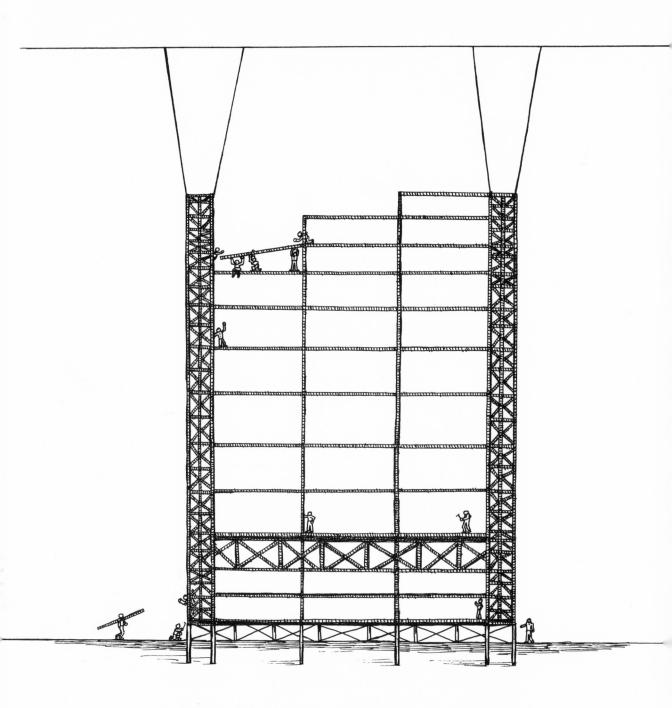

When each ring was finished, it was hung vertically next to
14   another and the cross-pieces were riveted into place.

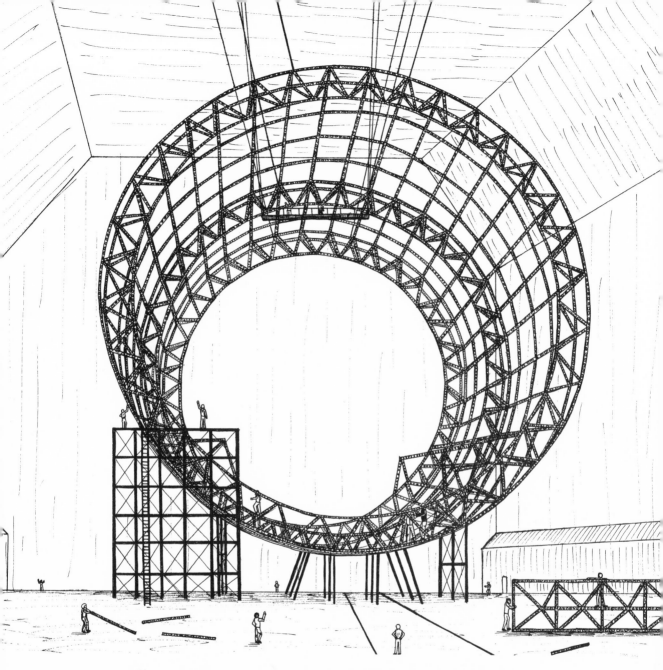

After several rings were riveted together, the airship began
to take shape. The tops of the rings were attached to the ceiling
with cables; the bottoms of the rings were braced with wooden
poles. Scaffolding was built alongside the airship so the
workers could reach all the parts.

15

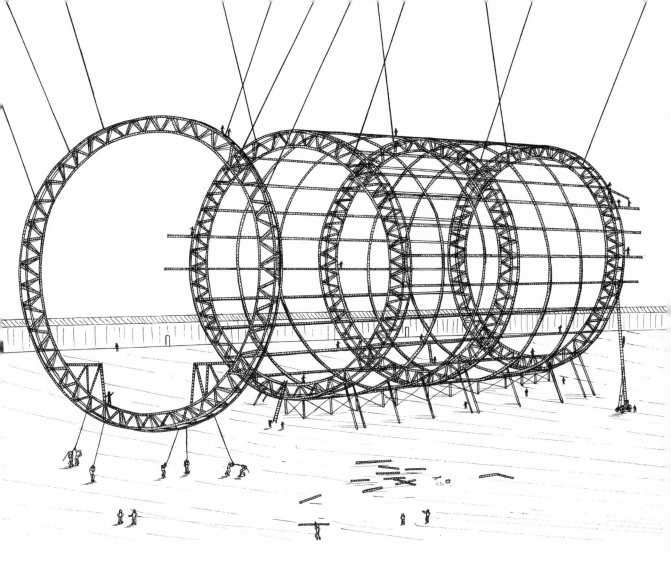

Long ladders were set in place. Narrower rings were also
16 built in place between the main rings.

At the same time, work began on the nose of the dirigible, which was built vertically. It soon resembled the frame of a giant tent.

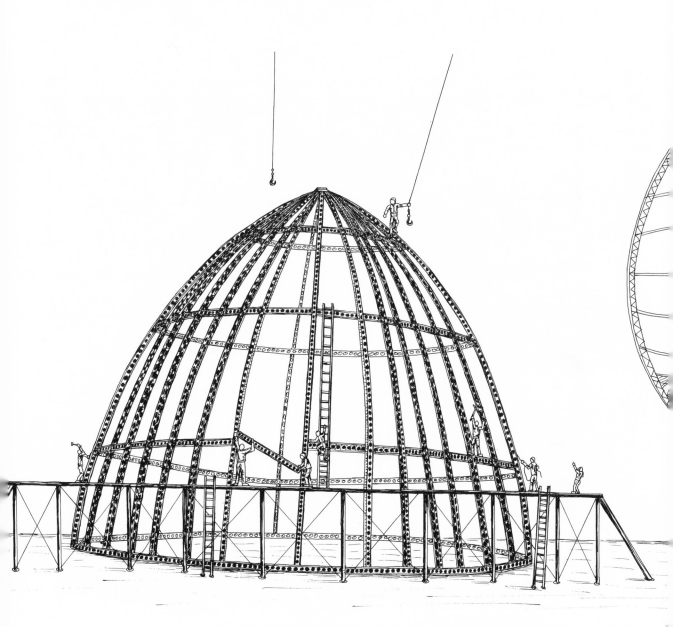

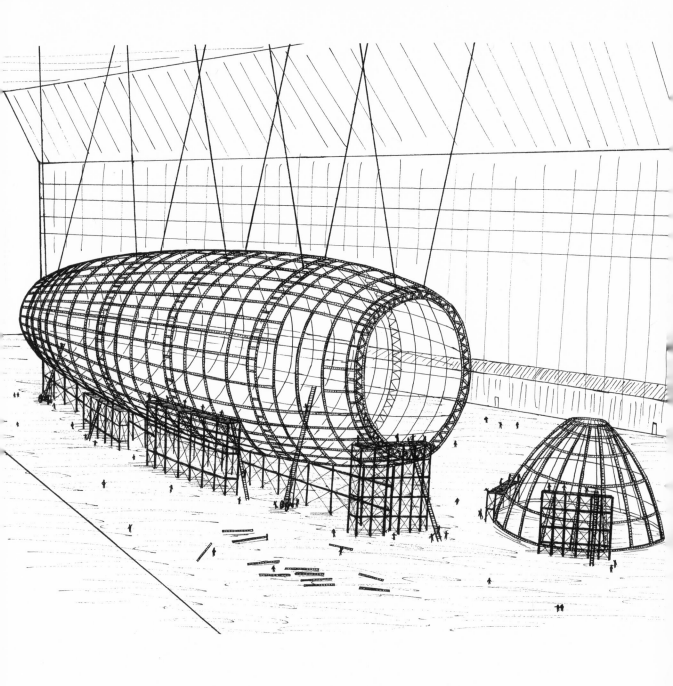

When the nose was completed, it would be raised and
18 riveted in place on the main body of the airship.

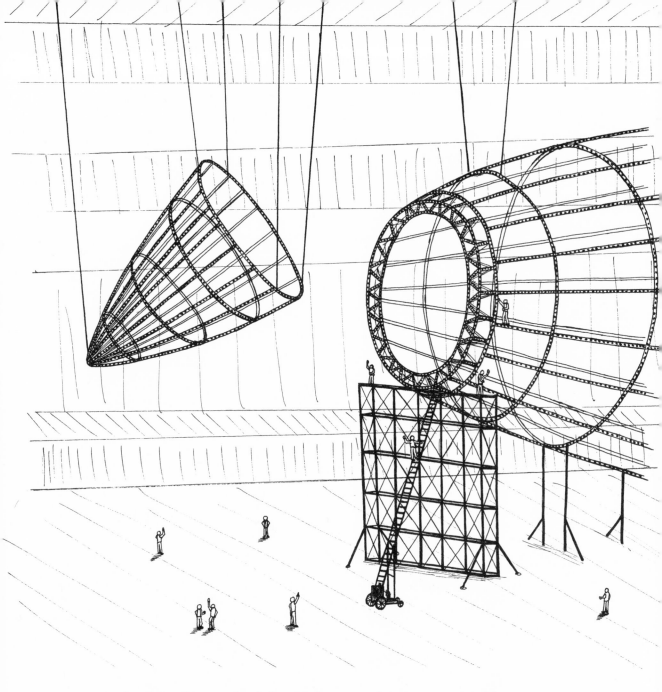

At the other end of the airship, workmen were building the tail and fins.

When the tail was finished, it, too, was raised and hung in place. It was then riveted to the main body. **19**

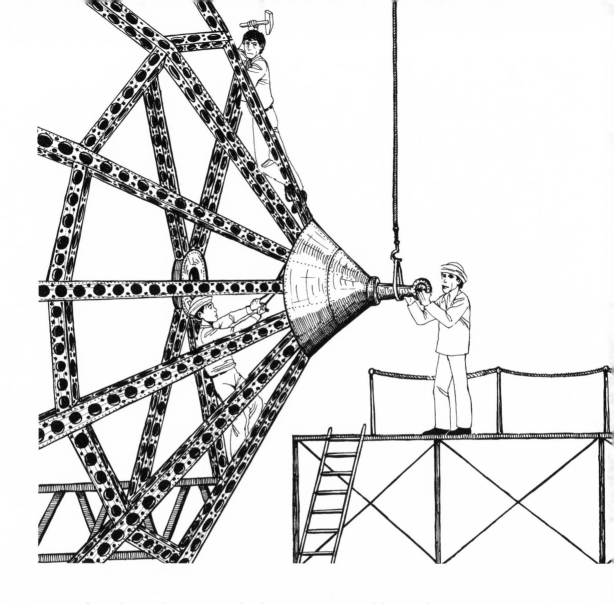

After the tail was attached, a person could stand on a walkway that ran down the middle of the airship and look all the way back to the end! The main framework was complete. Long girders ran from the nose of the ship all the way back to the tail. Workmen could now stand on the walkways inside the airship to finish the construction.

A special mooring cone was attached to the nose of the airship so that it would be able to dock at a mooring mast.

21

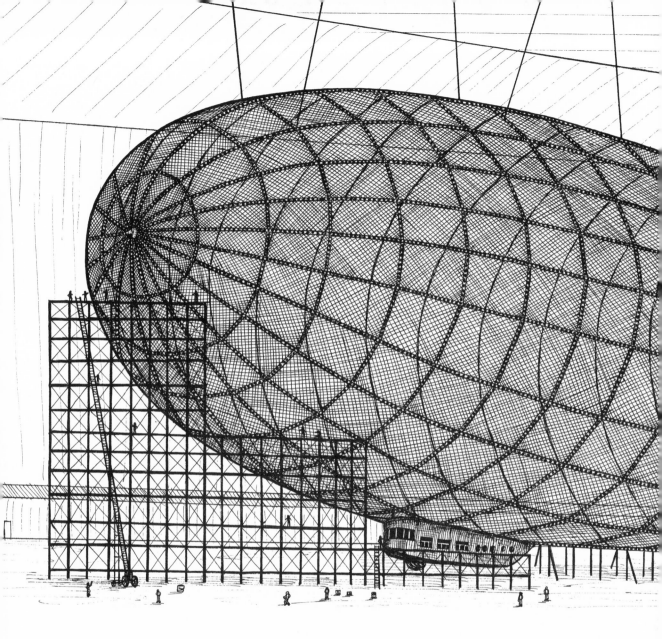

When the framework was completed, workmen on the ladders and scaffolding strung wire netting across the girders.

This netting would hold the gas cells in place and, later, the outer fabric would be stretched over it. Soon, the entire airship was covered with wire netting.

The control car, built separately, was also installed.

23

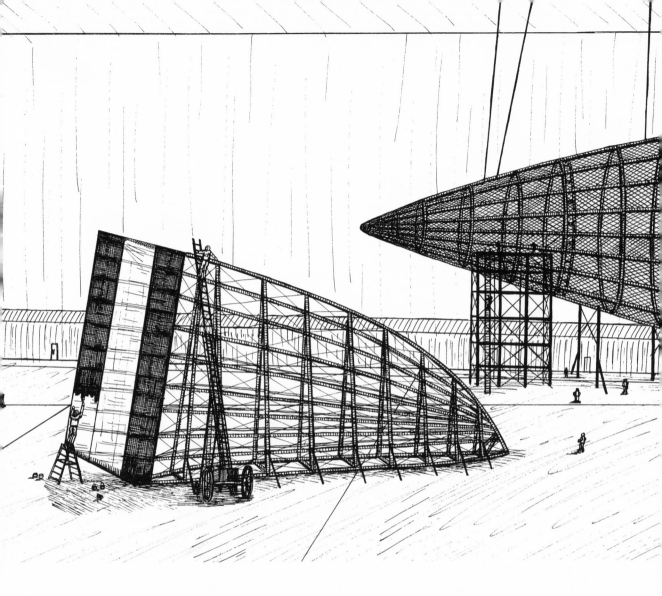

At the same time, the four fins were finished and covered with fabric. The rudders were then painted red, white and blue.

After the framework was covered with the netting, the outer fabric, made of cotton, was placed over everything. The pieces were sewn together with heavy cord.

Since it was a Naval airship, "U.S. Navy" was painted on **24** its side.

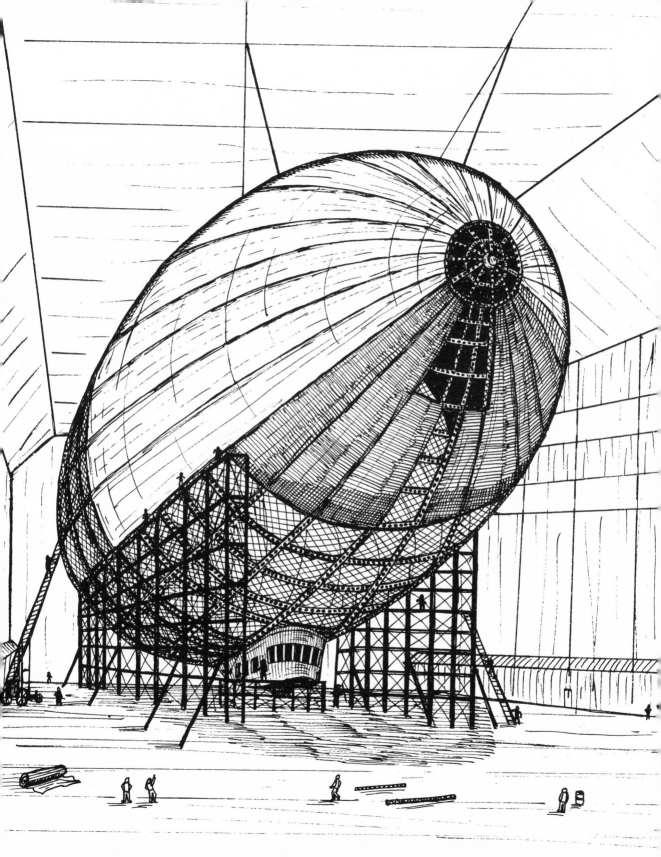

The fabric was sewn on in many separate sections. Workers inside the framework helped to fasten it in place.

In another part of the airship base, many women were constructing the gas cells. They sewed together pieces of rubberized fabric that were then varnished to make them airtight so that the helium could not leak out of the cells.

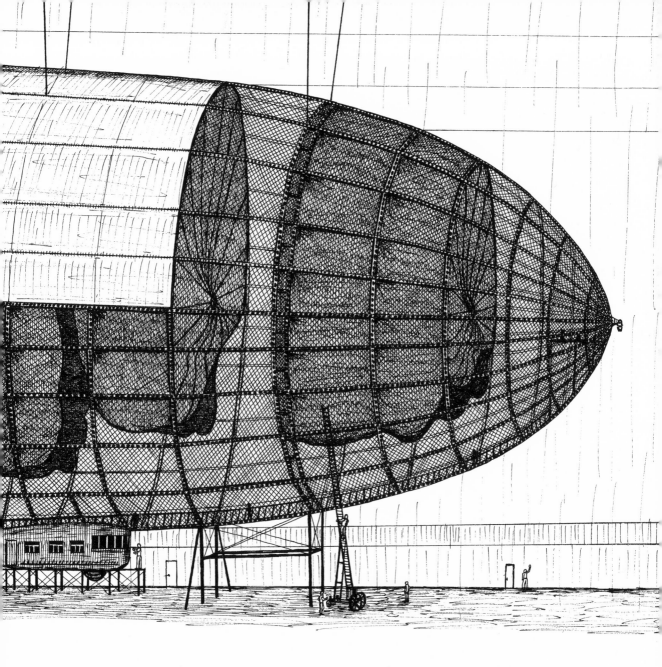

When the cells were finished they were placed inside the airship's frame. There were ten separate gas cells from the nose of the dirigible to its tail. They were made separately for safety reasons. In case a cell was damaged and lost its gas, the others would remain intact and the airship could continue to fly.

27

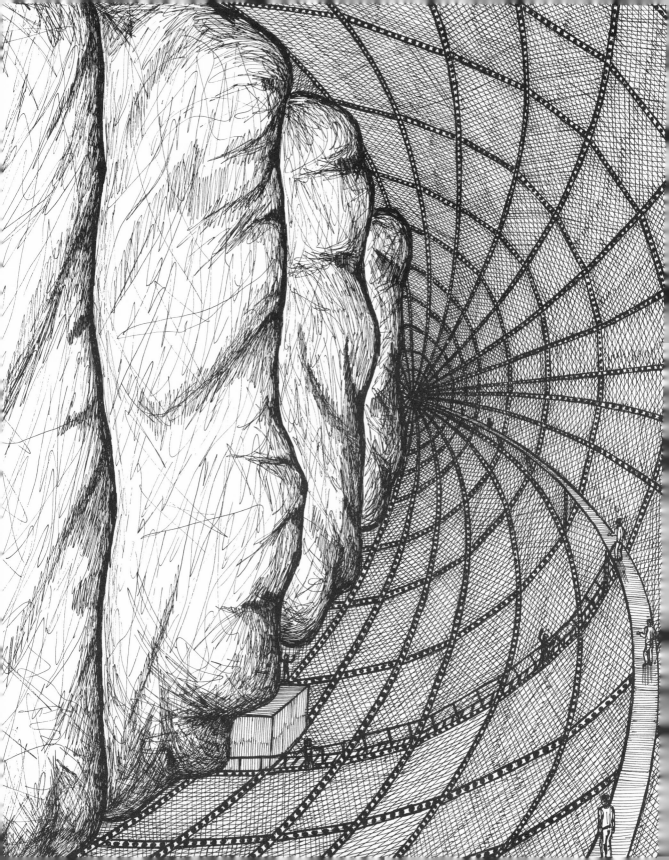

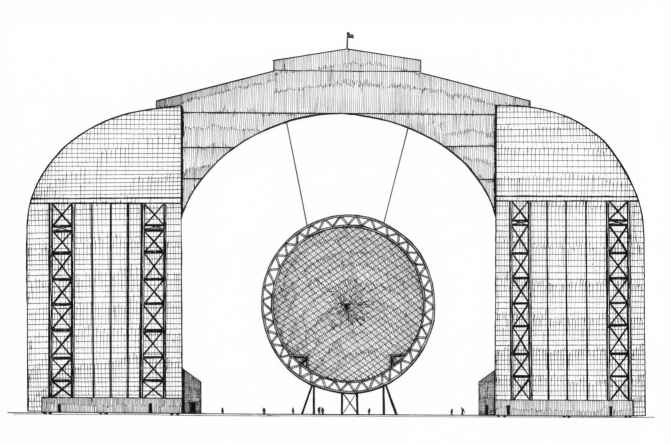

At first the gas cells were just hung inside the frame. They were not yet filled with gas.

Here is a crosssection of the dirigible inside its huge hangar. It had its cells in place, held firmly by the wire netting, but they were not yet filled with helium, so the airship was still supported by cables and bracing. The two enormous hangar doors on tracks were operated by motors.

When the four fins were completed, they were also raised

and riveted into place.

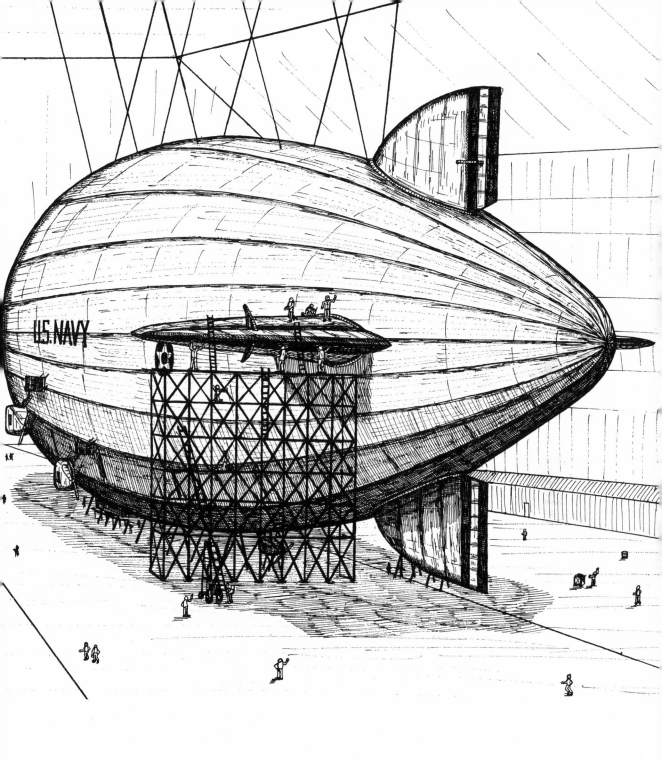

Workers could climb on the fins to finish attaching them.   **31**

At the same time, the five engine gondolas were being built. Inside each gondola was a powerful twelve-cylinder six-hundred-horsepower engine! The engine had a propeller attached to it by a long shaft. When the gondolas were completed they were riveted to the outside of the airship with aluminum bracing. There was enough room within the gondola for two crewmen—to check the engine and, if necessary, repair it while the airship was in flight.

A few months later, the airship was nearly all covered with the sections of fabric and all the engine gondolas were attached.

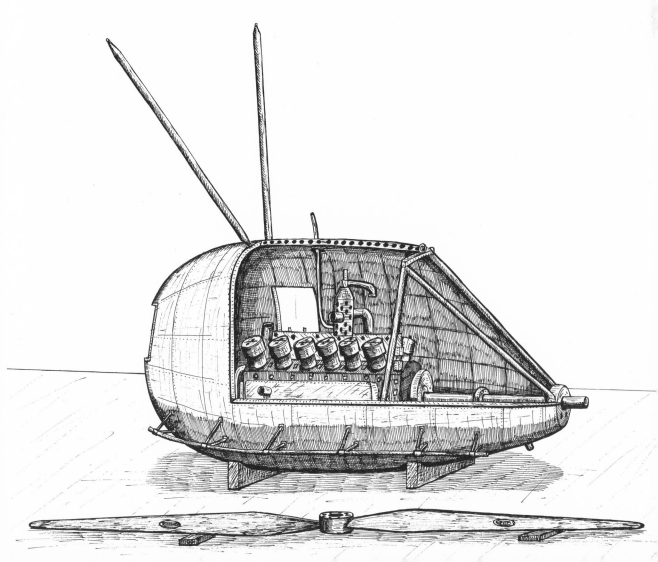

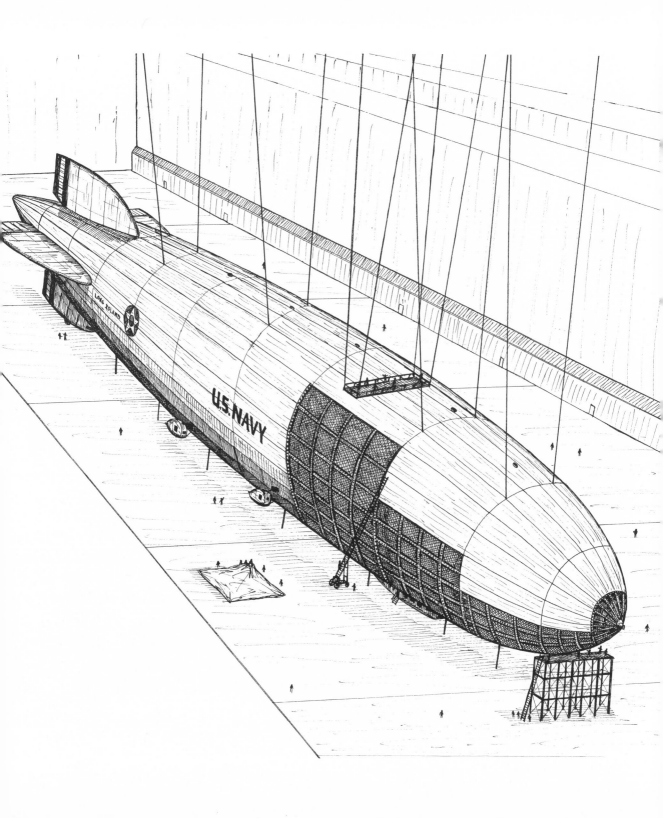

At long last, the final piece of fabric was sewn in place. The dirigible was then painted silver. The silver color reflected the sunlight, keeping the airship cool inside. When it flew, it looked like a great silver fish, a ship of the sky.

The new airship was then named the *Long Island*, honoring the place where it was built.

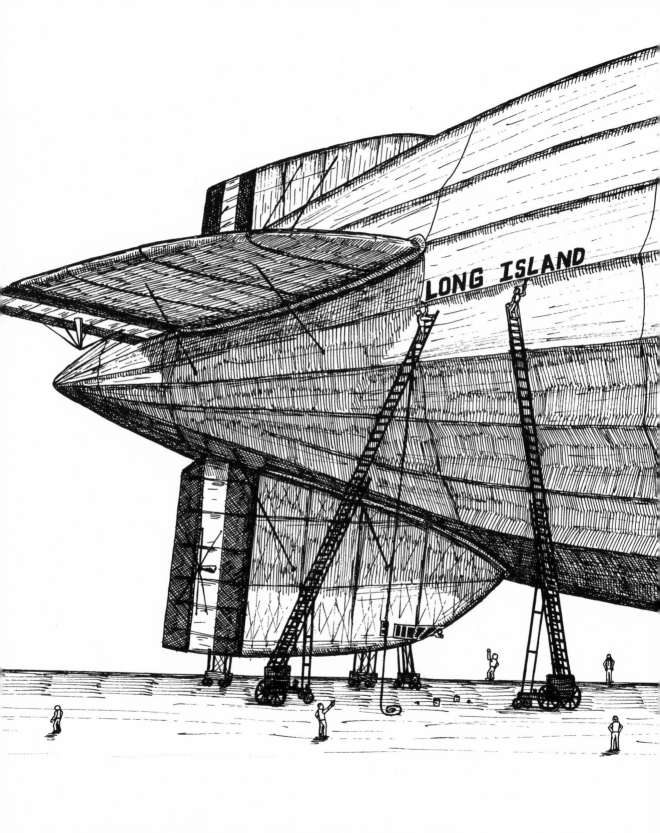

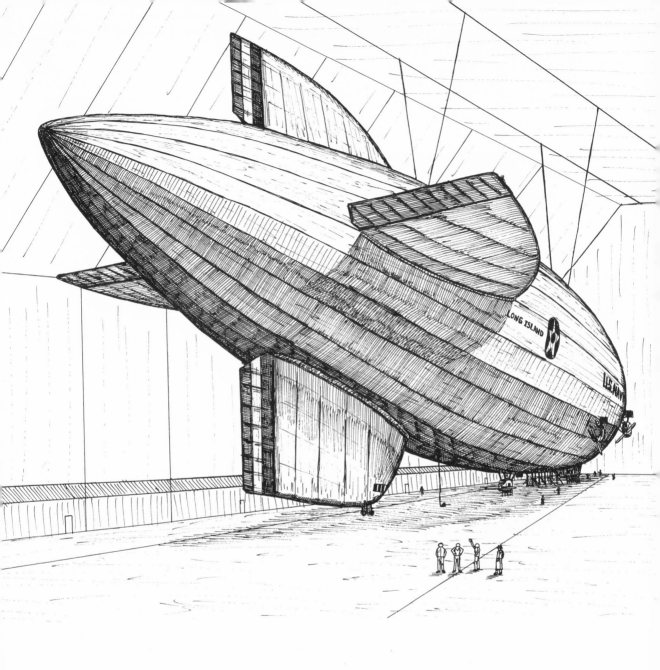

By late 1924, the dirigible was completed and braced in the
hangar, waiting to be filled with gas. People came to marvel at
36   the airship.

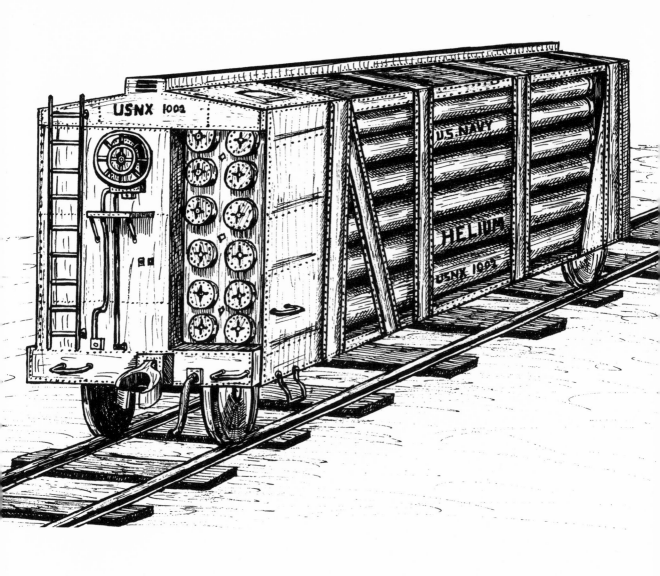

38   Soon, the helium gas arrived by train.

It was purified and pumped through hoses into the airship's gas cells. When the dirigible was filled with the gas, it could float by itself, so the cables and bracings were removed.

The big day arrived! The airship was completed! There was a special ceremony and a huge crowd of people came from all over to see this new lighter-than-air craft.

Important people made speeches, a band played, photographers took pictures, and a lady christened the dirigible. The *Long Island* was now ready for its first flight.

The dirigible was attached to a motorized mooring mast, which pulled it out of the hangar.

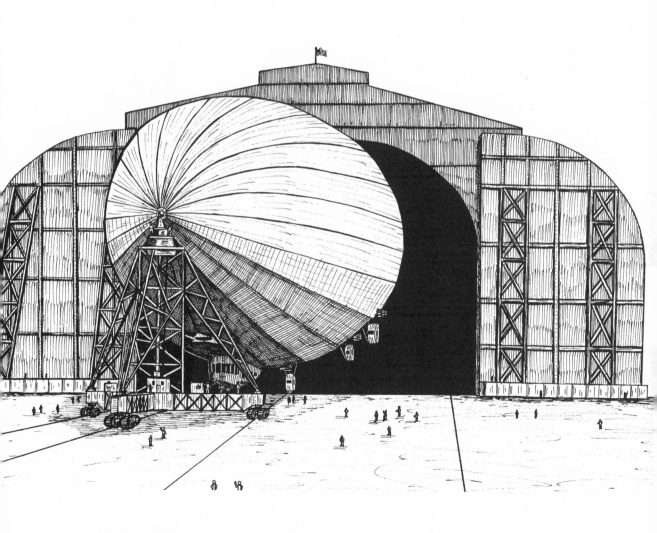

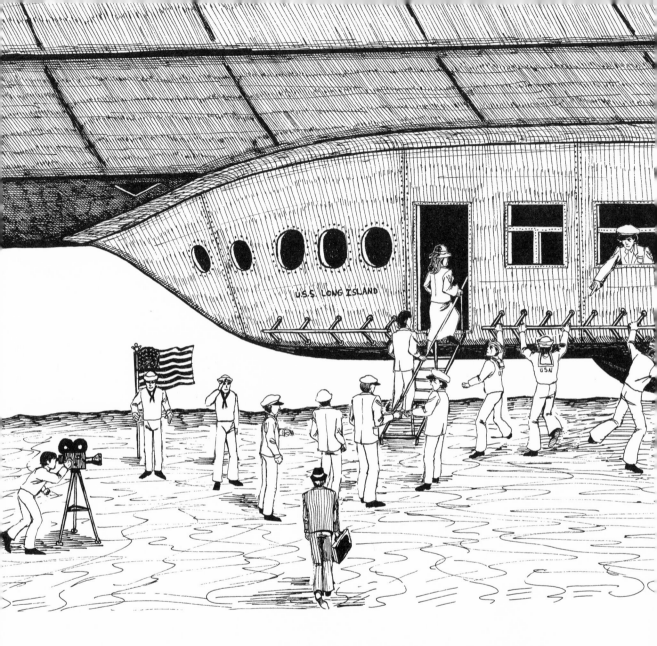

Many important people and dignitaries boarded the airship for its first flight. Ground crewmen, holding railings, steadied the dirigible as it was now floating just above the ground. The passengers remained in the control car, which was the nerve center of the ship. The captain and officers were there, too.

44

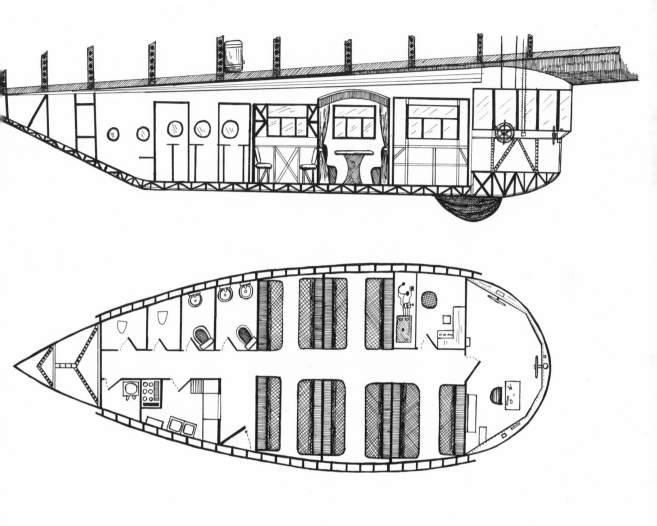

Located in the front of the control car were all the instruments and controls for the airship. The center and back of the control car had passenger seats, tables, bathrooms and a kitchen. There were windows all around so that everyone could look out.

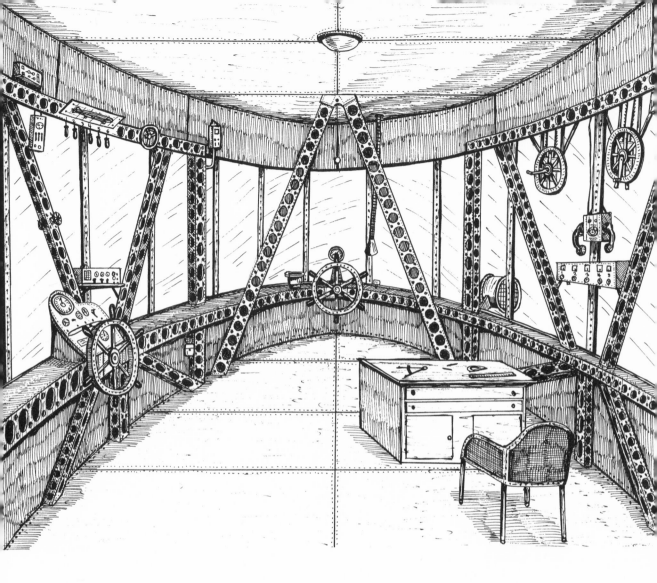

The officers and crewmen steered the airship by means of
a control wheel at the front of the car, which turned the rudder
to the left or right. A second wheel on the left side pointed the
nose up or down by moving the elevators. Above this wheel
were handles to dump water ballast. On the right side were two
46 handles to regulate the engines and other controls to release

gas. Telephones were connected to other parts of the huge airship. The navigator worked at the desk to plot the course and position of the dirigible.

When it was time to launch the airship, the captain shouted, "Up Ship!" Water ballast was dumped to make the ship lighter.

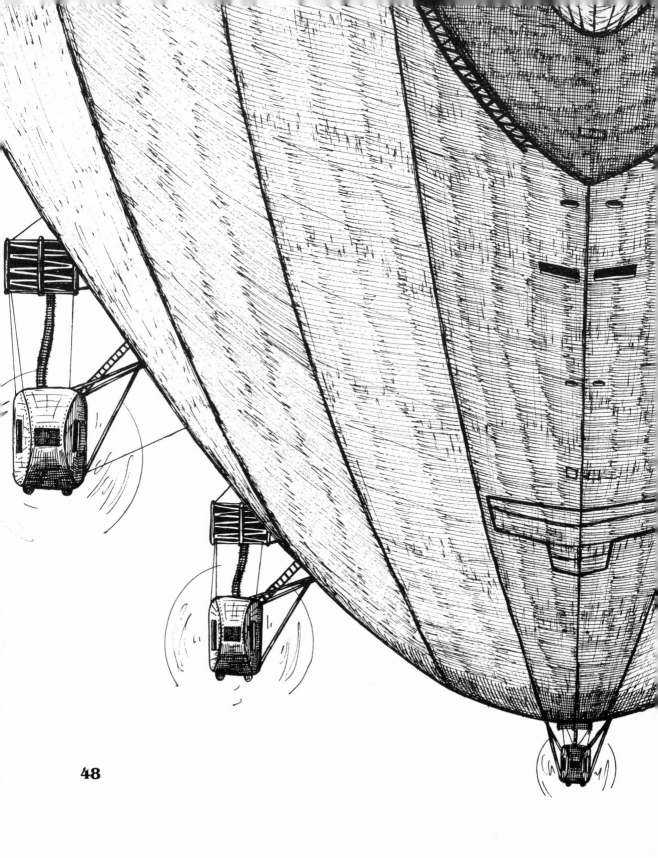

48

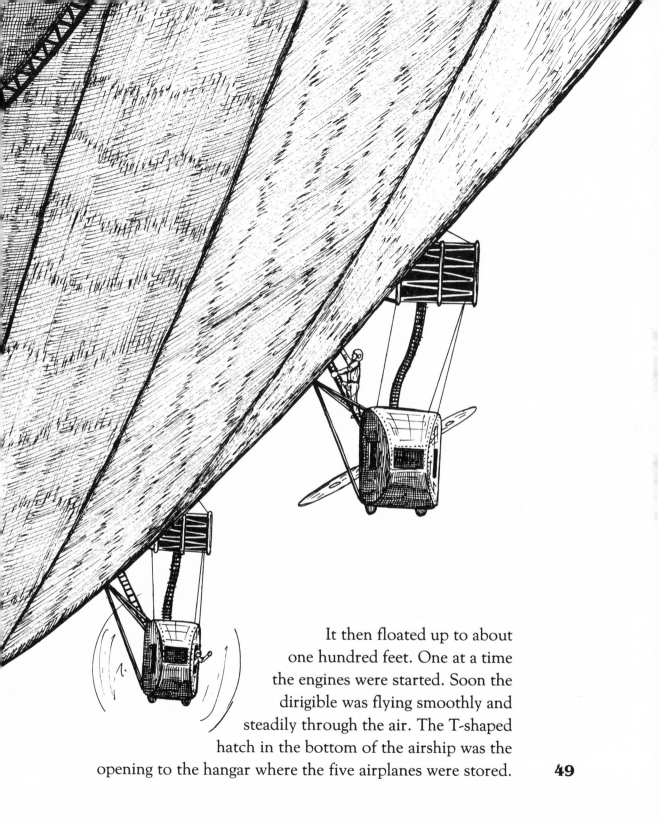

It then floated up to about one hundred feet. One at a time the engines were started. Soon the dirigible was flying smoothly and steadily through the air. The T-shaped hatch in the bottom of the airship was the opening to the hangar where the five airplanes were stored.

49

The thirty passengers inside, like all the other passengers on later flights, had a very smooth ride. They sat in comfortable surroundings and ate wonderful meals. The flight was so smooth that nothing on the table moved even an inch. The passengers dined elegantly while watching the world pass serenely beneath the windows.

50   The view was breath-taking from inside the dirigible!

Porters saw to the passengers' every need.

The seats could be turned into comfortable beds for sleeping.

On its first flight, the airship flew from its Long Island base to New York City. Everyone in the city stopped whatever they were doing to watch the huge dirigible sail majestically overhead. People honked their car horns and ships in the harbor blew their whistles.

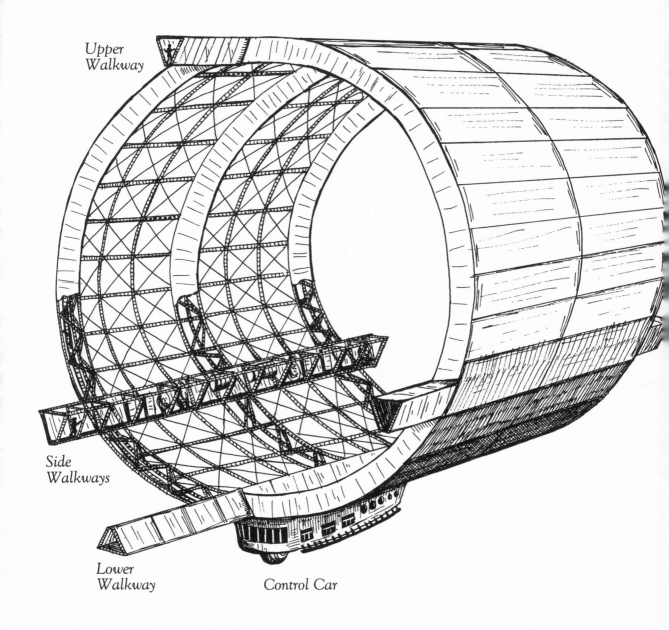

Upper
Walkway

Side
Walkways

Lower
Walkway

Control Car

Meanwhile, inside the airship, the fifty crewmen went
about their duties. There were walkways and electric lights all
54   through the dirigible.

There was even a ladder inside the curved nose (bow). This ladder was surrounded by gas cells and water ballast tanks.

Crewmen had to be careful when climbing this ladder because beneath them was only the thin outer fabric, and then a very long fall.

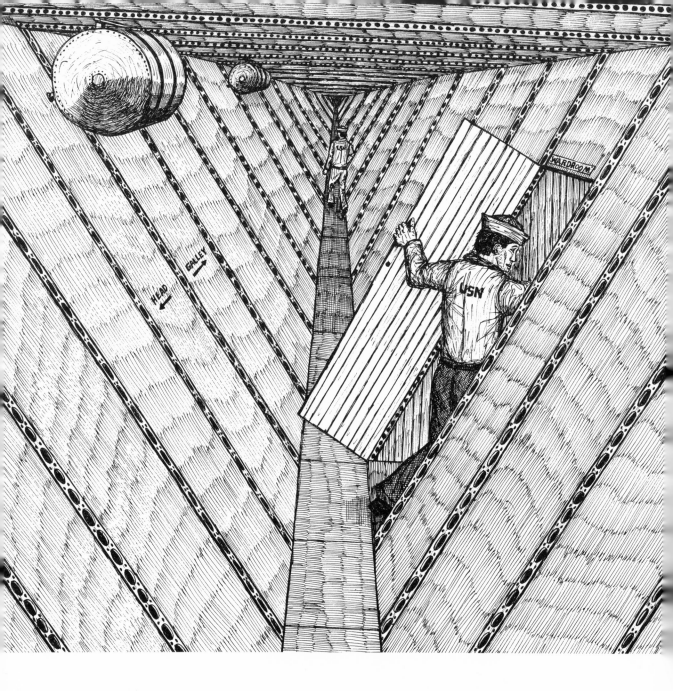

The main walkway was located along the interior of the bottom of the airship. It was very long and narrow and there were fuel tanks hanging above it. Other walkways were located on the sides and top. Doorways led from them to many rooms.

One of the rooms contained the crewmen's bathroom.

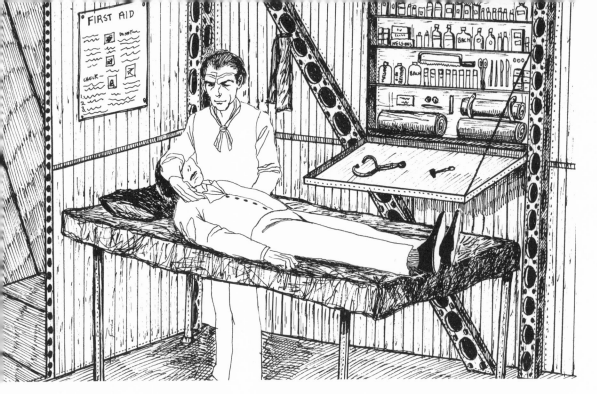

Another was the sickbay, in case someone became ill, or was injured.

The crewmen also had their own kitchen and lounge.

58

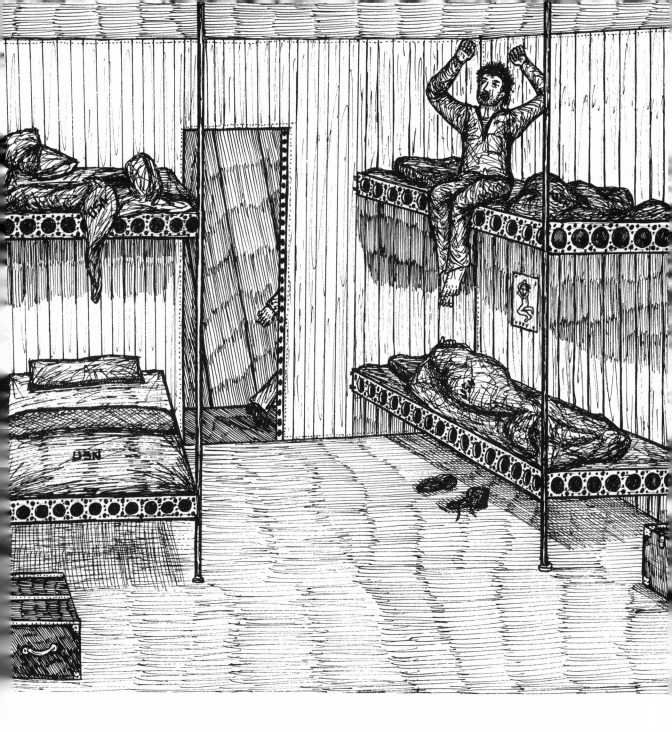

There were also sleeping quarters provided for them because the airship could fly for a week without landing.

Ladders led up to the top of the dirigible so that the crewmen could climb outside while they were flying. During one flight, a small rip developed in the fabric, and crewmen climbed outside and repaired it while the airship was moving. The circular openings on the top of the dirigible were gas valves to release helium.

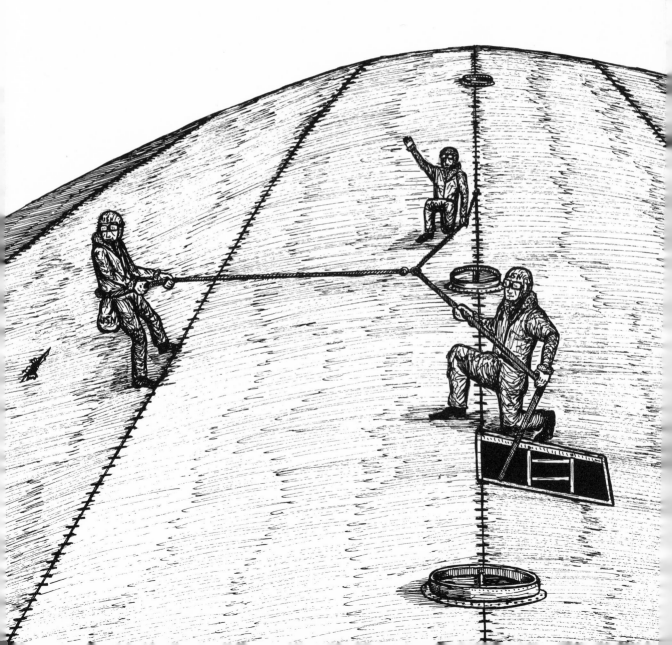

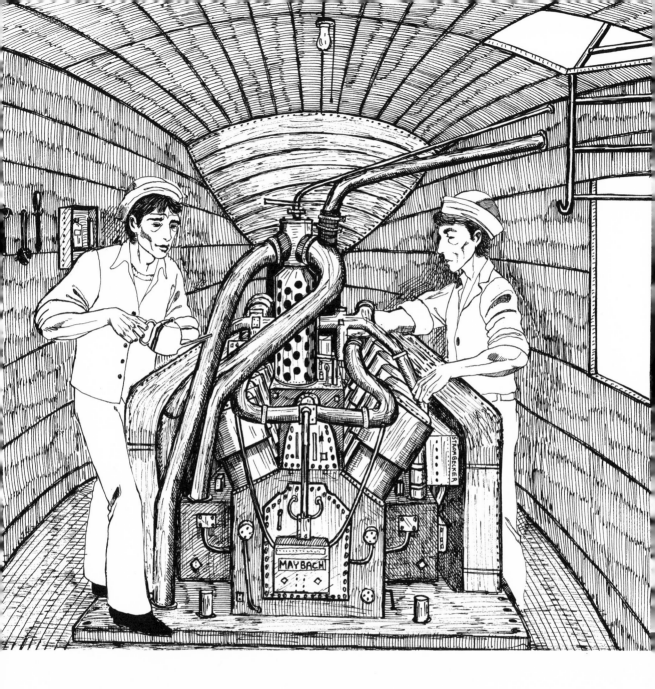

Whenever the airship was in flight, there was always at least one crewman inside each engine gondola. They would monitor the engine's performance and make any necessary repairs. It was a very noisy place to work.

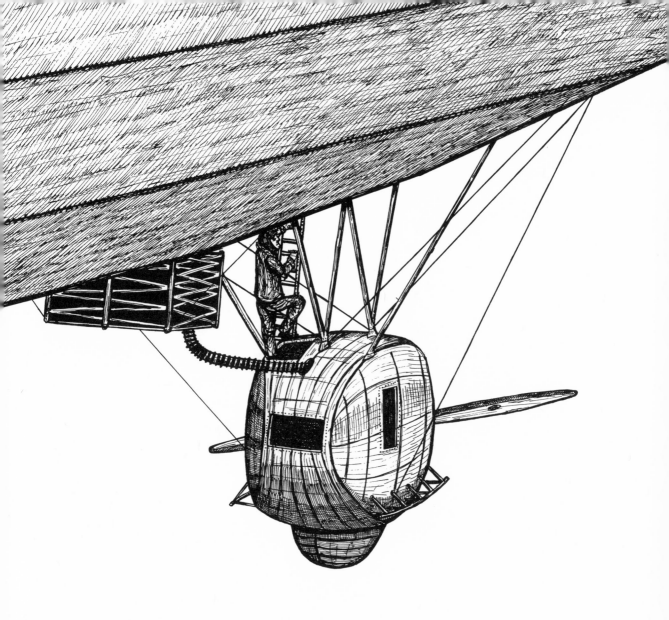

When changing shifts, the crewmen had to climb on an open ladder between the dirigible and the engine gondola. They had to be very careful not to slip because there were no safety

62 lines!

At the tail of the airship, crewmen could go inside the fins.
Inside the lower vertical fin was a secondary control area.
Crewmen climbed down a ladder to reach it.

This secondary control area was a backup, in case something went wrong inside the main control car. Two crewmen were always stationed there in case they were needed to steer the airship. They communicated by telephone to the control car.

For the first few landings, the *Long Island* just valved off some gas and descended to the airfield. Then it dropped several landing lines, which were held onto by about three hundred ground crewmen.

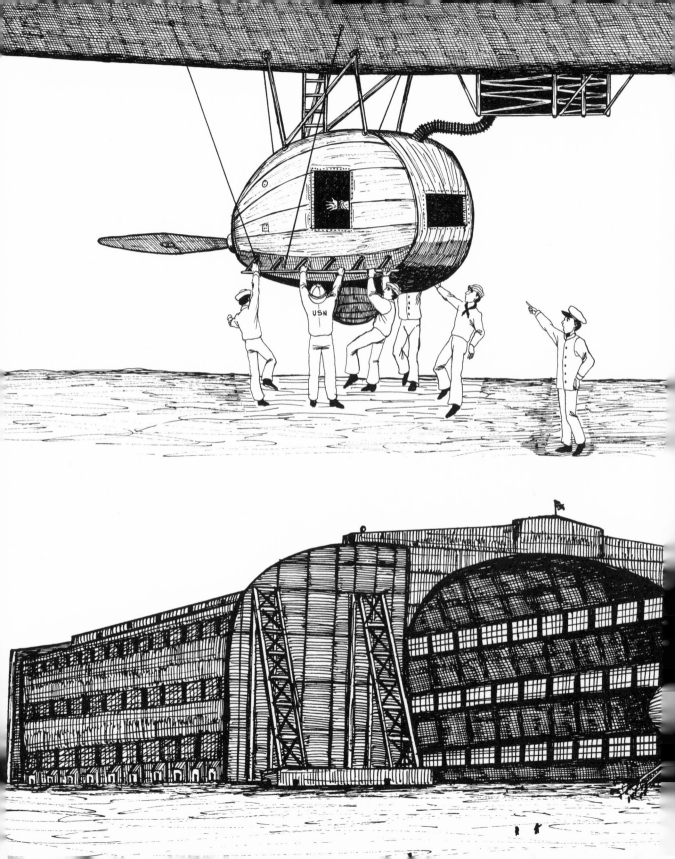

Other crewmen grabbed the railings on the control car and lower engine gondola.

They all held the airship close to the ground and then guided it inside the hangar. This was a difficult operation on a windy day. Once the ship was inside the hangar, the big doors were closed.

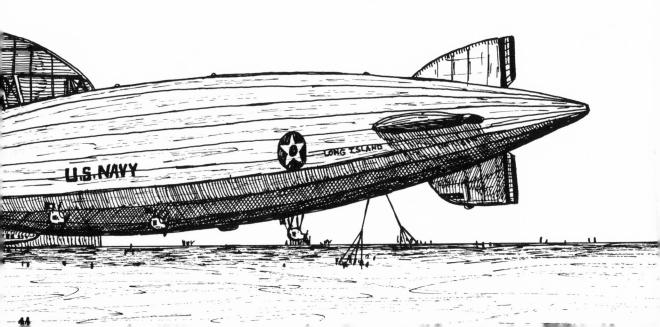

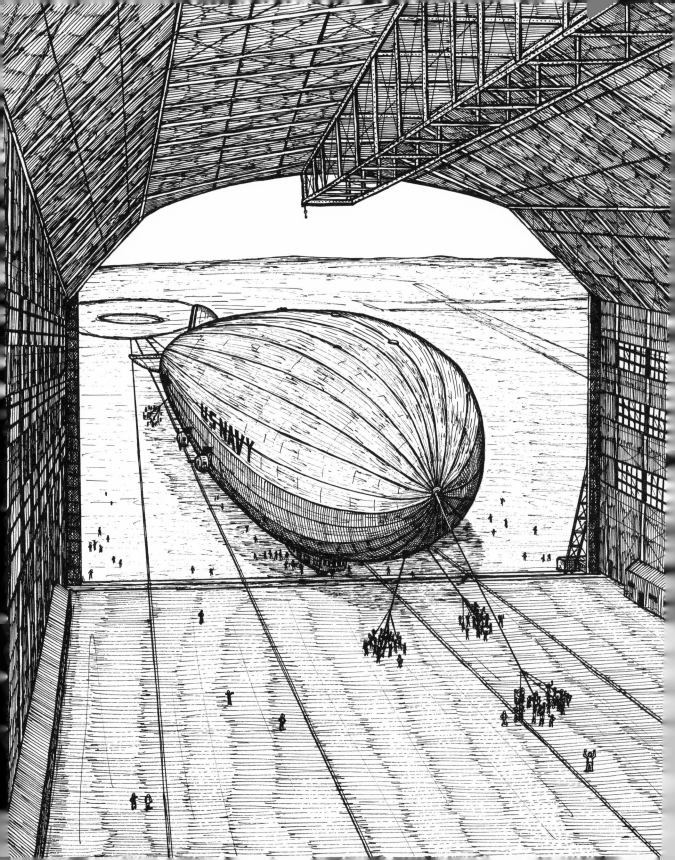

In the 1920s and 1930s the *Long Island* made many flights
all over America.   **69**

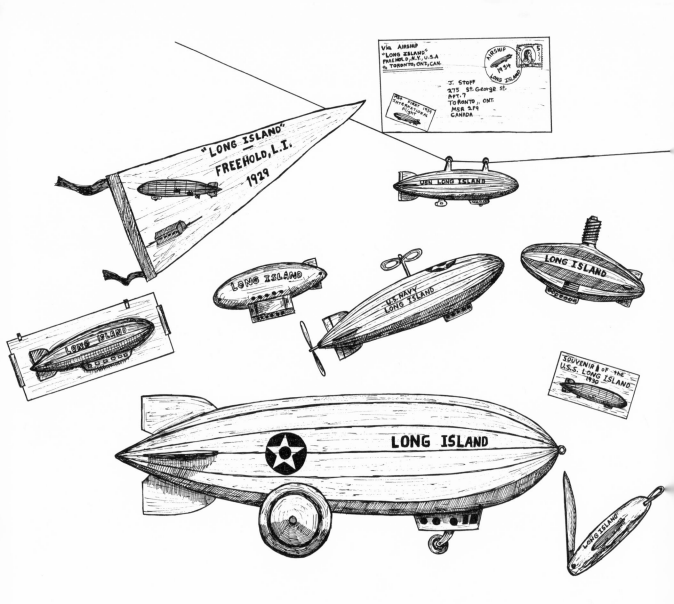

Soon everybody in the United States had either seen or read of the great dirigible. In a short time it had become very popular and there were many toys and souvenirs made of it. There were dirigible pull-toys, pocket knives, candy molds, harmonicas, wind-up toys, Christmas tree lights, pins, toys on strings, pennants and souvenir postal covers that had been flown on the airship.

Eventually, a new and easier method for landing the air-ship was perfected, using a mooring mast. When the dirigible reached the hangar, water ballast was dumped from its nose and a cable was lowered through the mooring cone.

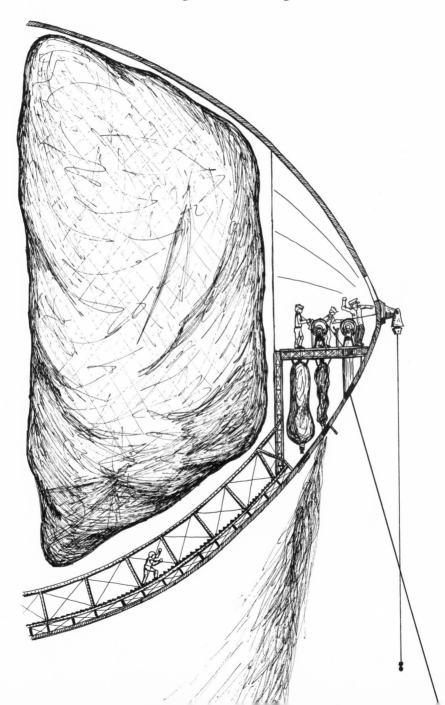

The ground crewmen on the mooring mast lowered a cable from the top of the mast.

The two cables were then connected on the ground and the mooring mast would reel in the airship like a giant silver fish. The nose of the airship locked into the top of the mooring mast.

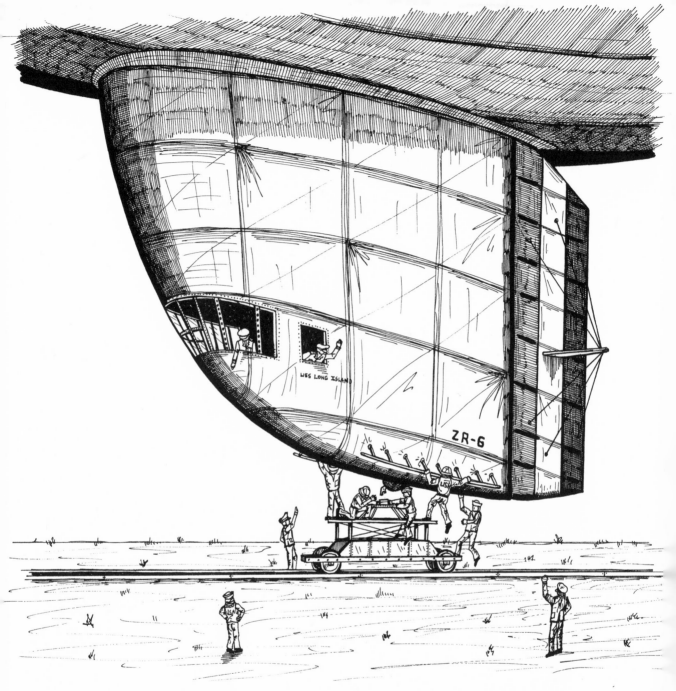

The lower vertical fin of the airship would then be attached to a dolly on tracks to hold the tail steady. Then the motorized mooring mast just pulled the airship inside the hangar.

At several other places in the nation, special two hundred foot tall mooring masts, called "high masts," were constructed. These masts could be used to service a dirigible without it ever entering a hangar.

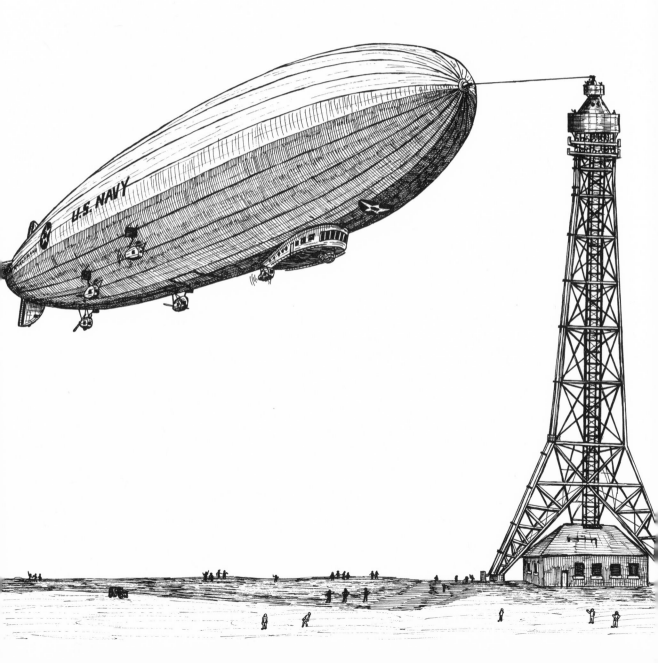

The airship was moored to these high masts in the same way as the shortened mooring mast. The cable from the airship's nose would be attached on the ground to the cable from the mast's top. It would then be reeled in and secured. After it was moored, a gangplank would be lowered from the dirigible's nose to the top of the mooring mast. Thus, crewmen and supplies could be transferred to the airship without it ever having to land.

An elevator ran from the ground to the top of the mooring mast. Lines and hoses were attached from the mast to the airship so that the airship could be replenished with fuel and helium. While the airship was moored to the top of the high mast, its tail would swing lazily in the breeze.

The *Long Island* often went on maneuvers with the Naval fleet. It was used as a long-range scout because it flew much farther than airplanes and could carry much more fuel. The crew communicated by radio to the ships at sea. Two small blimps, airships with no rigid framework, of ZF-1 squadron escorted it out to sea.

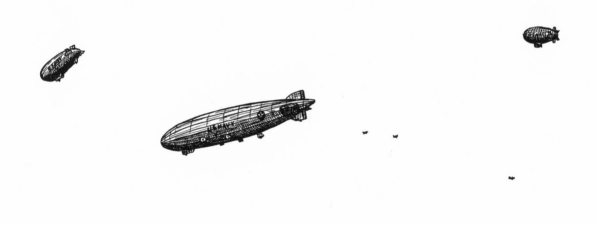

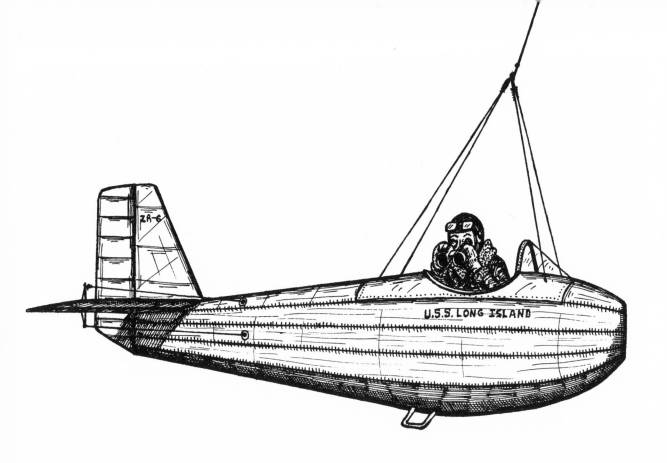

The *Long Island* also had a special, streamlined observation car called the "cloud car." The airship could stay high above the clouds and lower an observer in the cloud car about a thousand feet on a steel cable. This observer communicated what he saw, via telephone, to the airship above. Since the airship could stay above the clouds where it could not be seen from sea or land, an observer in the cloud car could watch an enemy without detection, because the car was so small and far away.

On maneuvers, the *Long Island* launched and recovered its five fighter planes in flight. The five planes were Curtiss F9C Sparrowhawks and they were carried inside the airship in a hangar. After launching and going on patrol, the planes would return to the airship. They reduced their air speed to that of the airship's—about eighty miles per hour.

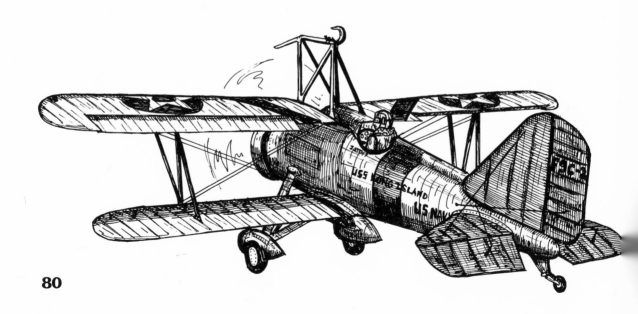

Then they flew underneath the airship and aligned them-
selves with a "trapeze" that had been lowered from the ship. **81**

An officer inside the airship would sometimes give directions to the pilots to help them with the alignment.

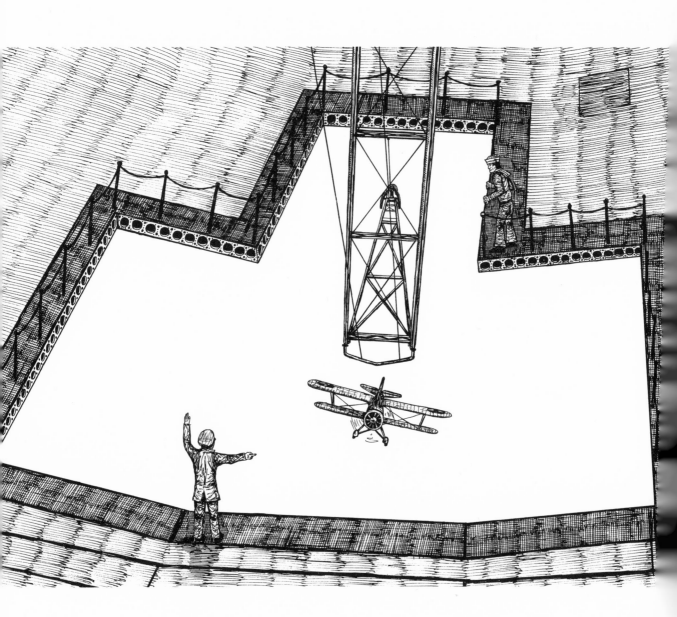

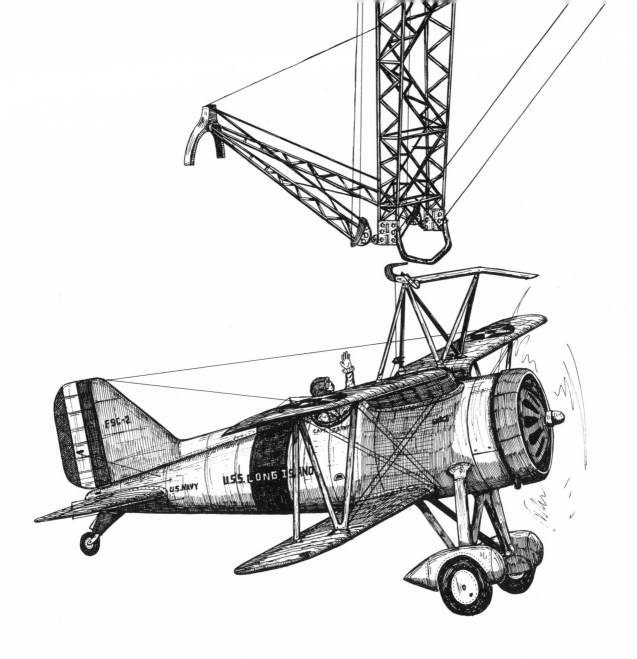

The pilots would try to catch onto the bar of the trapeze with the hooks above the wings on the airplanes. When the hook was caught, they pulled a handle that locked the hook securely on the bar.

The guide bar on the trapeze would then lower and lock onto the fuselage of the airplane to hold it steady.

The whole trapeze with the airplane attached was raised
inside the hangar of the airship.

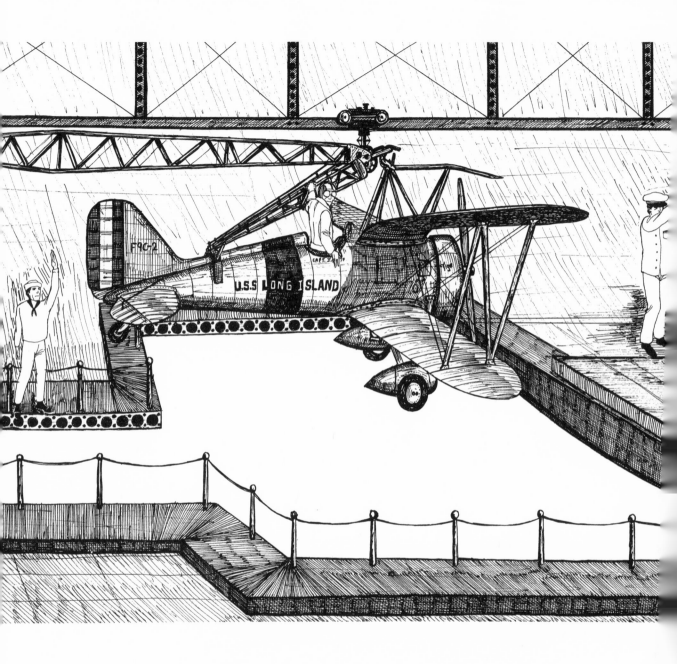

Once fully raised, the airplane was transferred to an over-head dolly and pulled out of the way to make room to recover the next airplane. Although it sounds tricky, the pilots quickly got used to the operation.

Here is the *Long Island* flying over the cruiser *Ithaca*, the aircraft carrier CV 4 *Ranger*, the airship tender *Yonge* and several smaller ships, while a Grumman FF-1 fighter passes nearby. This is how it would have looked from an airplane flying above the dirigible.

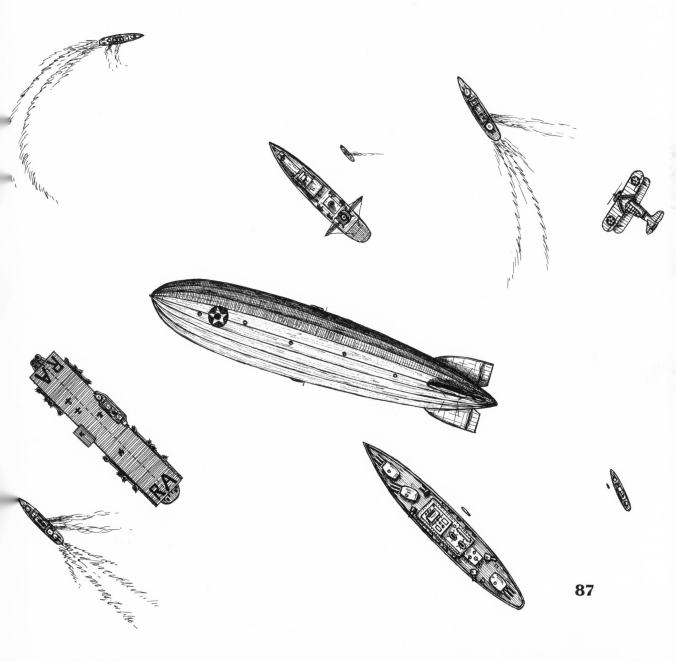

A few times, the airship landed on the deck of the aircraft carrier, *Ranger*, to transfer supplies.

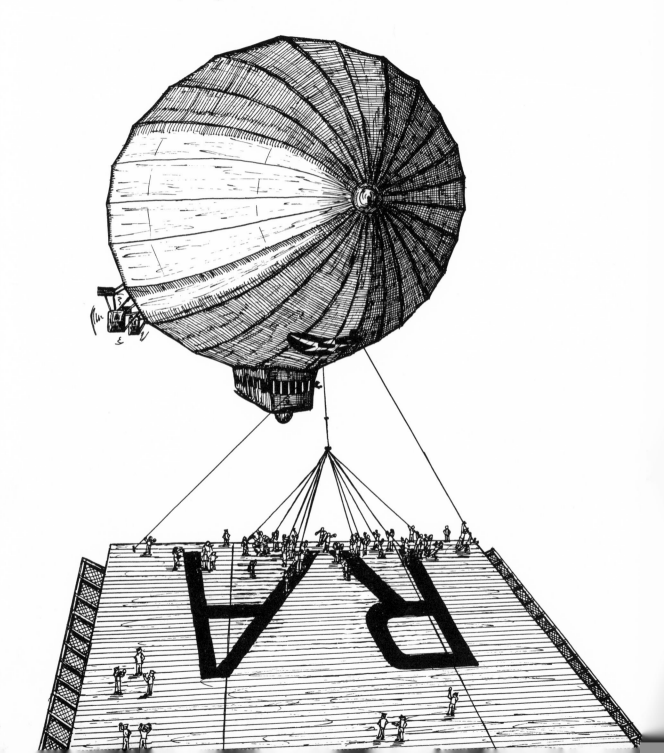

The Navy also modified an oiler to make it an airship tender. This ship, the U.S.S. *Yonge*, had a mooring mast built on it so that the airship could moor to it at sea and replenish its supplies. This meant that the *Long Island* could fly for even longer periods without ever having to go to its airship base on shore.

Mooring to the ship was just like mooring to the high mast: the dirigible was just reeled in. Once fully reeled in, its nose was locked in place at the top of the mast, but its tail could still swing freely.

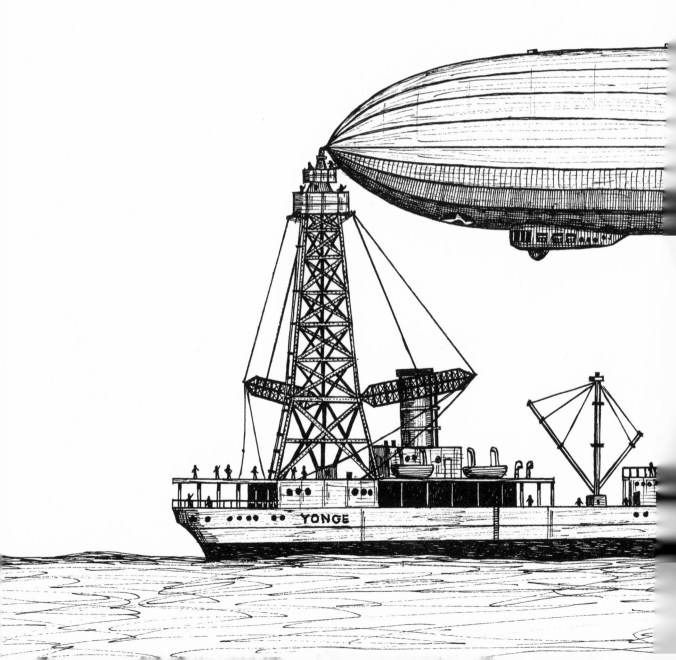

This was an impressive sight! The *Long Island* was about the same size as the *Yonge*!

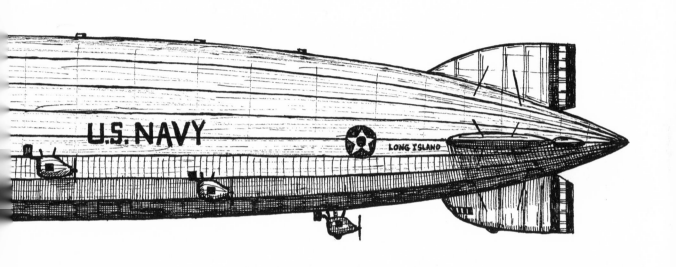

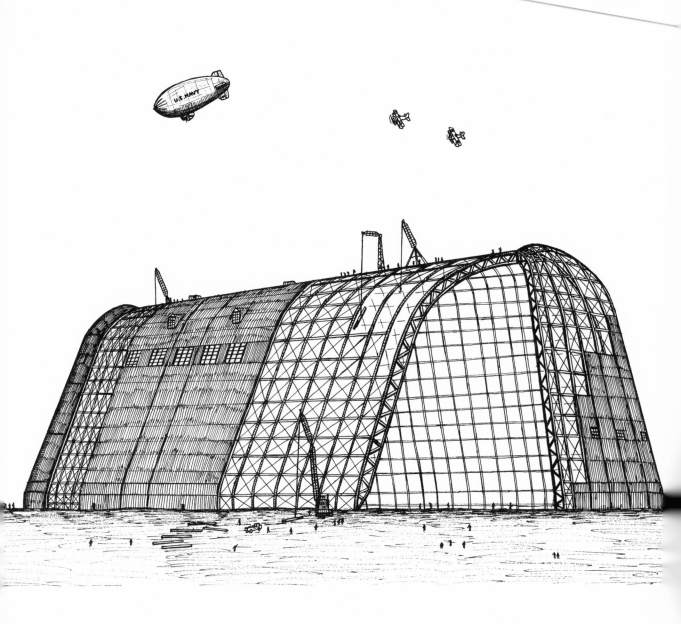

In the early 1930's, a new airship base was built on the West Coast at Marshak Field, near San Francisco. To house the *Long Island*, a huge new hangar was built. Now the airship had bases on both coasts of the United States. This new field also had a mobile mooring mast and the dirigible landed there many times.

Often, the *Long Island* had to dump a great deal of water ballast when it was landing. This certainly made the airship lighter, but it also gave the groundcrew a bath!

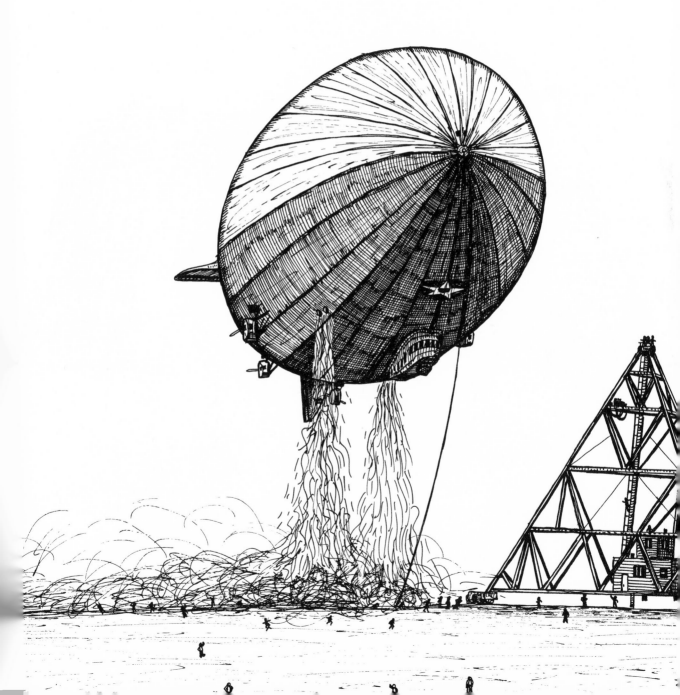

The hangar at Marshak Field was more cylindrical than the one at Freehold, and it had huge clamshell doors. When the *Long Island* landed here it always attracted an enormous crowd.

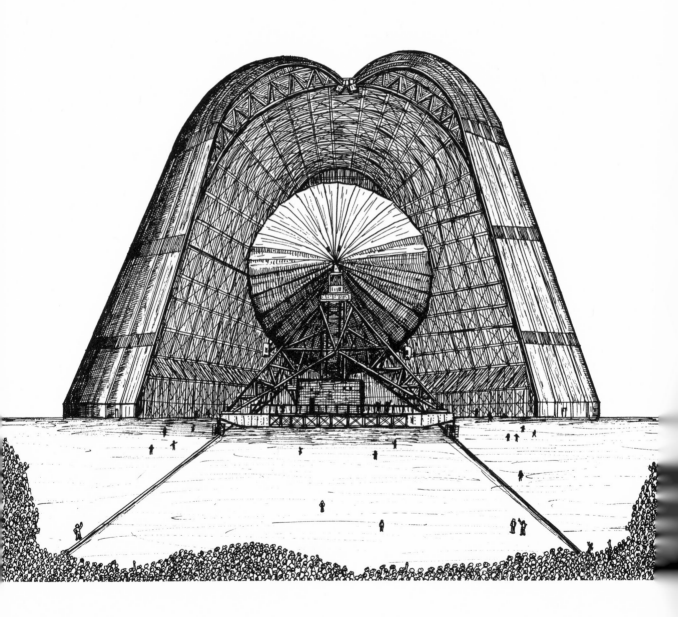

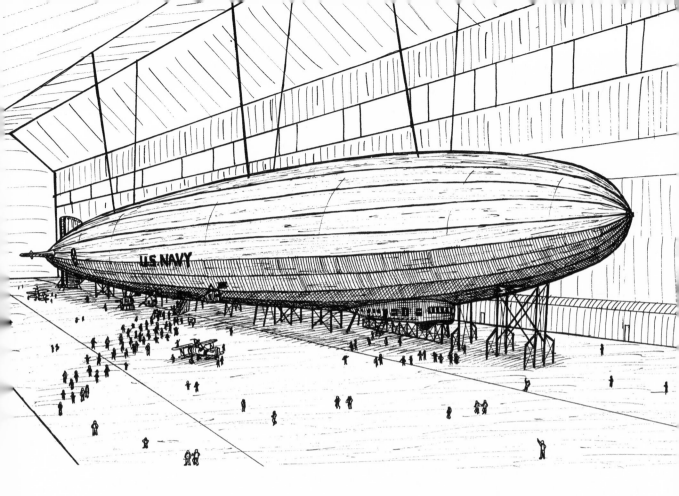

The *Long Island* was based at Marshak Field for a few years; but, it was pulled out of its hangar for the last time in 1938. It flew back to its birthplace at Freehold.

The U.S. Government and the Navy decided that they no longer needed rigid airships. They believed that they were too expensive to operate and were unnecessary. It was a sad decision for many.

Throughout 1939 and into 1940, the *Long Island* sat unwanted in its hangar at Freehold. Its helium was removed and, once again, it was hung by cables and braces. Because it was America's last rigid airship, it was made into a museum and thousands of people came to see it.

Tours were given of all parts of the airship and people took
pictures and bought souvenirs.

In 1940, the Navy decided that the airship took up too much room. They wanted to store airplanes and small blimps in the hangar. So they gave the order to dismantle the *Long Island* and sell it for scrap. In fact, the Navy ordered that nothing at all should be saved—not even for museums. Many people then did not like the decision and many more regret it today.

First the outer fabric was ripped off.

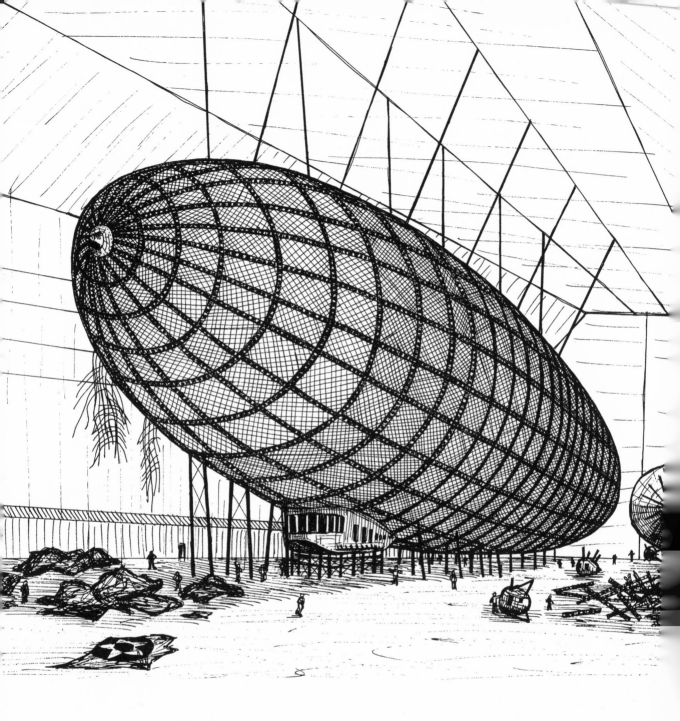

Then, the wire netting, fins, gas cells and engine gondolas were removed.

Then the aluminum girders were chopped off and piled up.

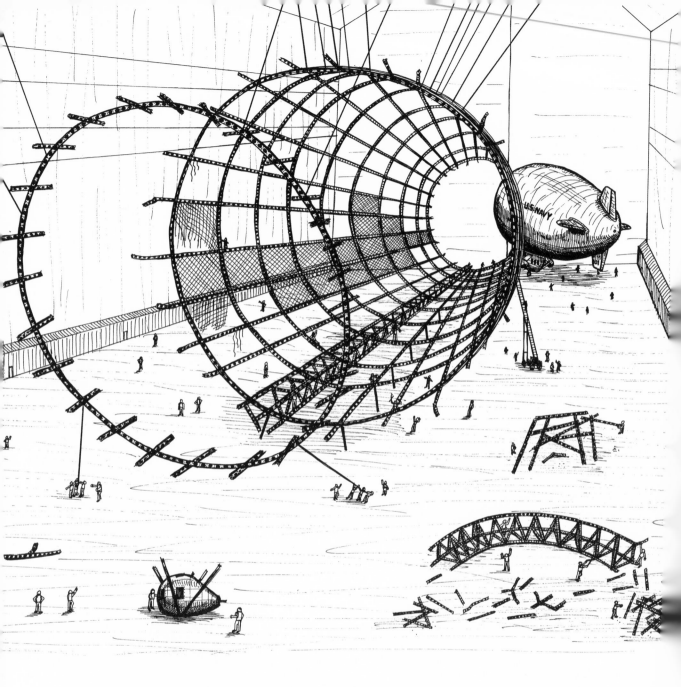

Finally, the main rings were separated, lowered and disassembled on the ground. The Navy was now storing the smaller airships, blimps, in the hangar. For the next twenty-five years they used these blimps successfully.

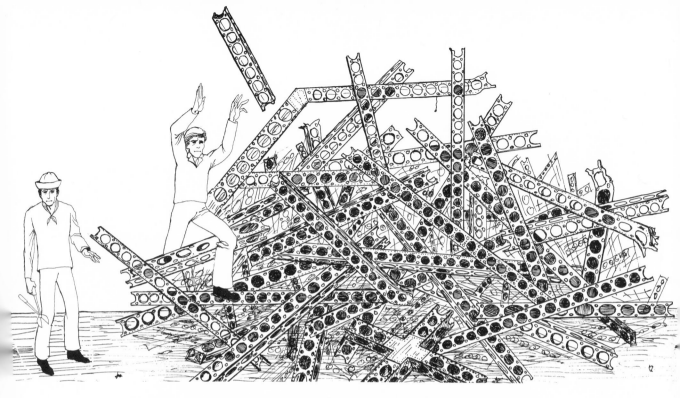

In the end, the few remaining large pieces of the *Long Island* were chopped up, piled up, and sold for scrap metal.

A few pieces were rescued. Some are in museums today.

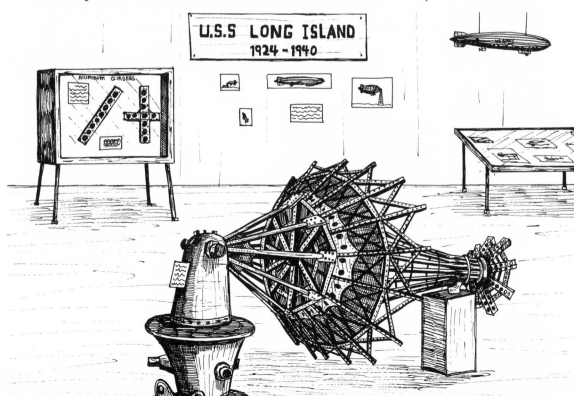

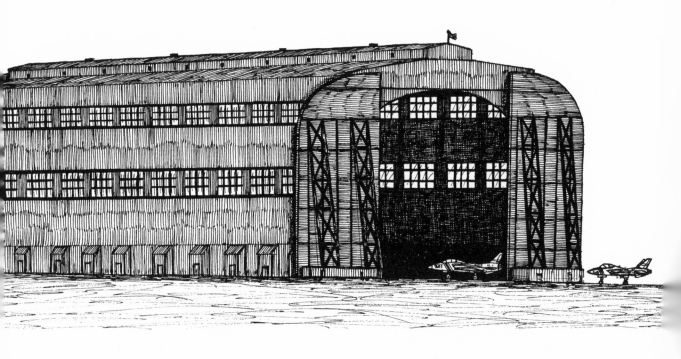

The hangar at Freehold is still in existence and the Navy now stores Grumman F-14's in it. Whenever one of the Goodyear blimps is in the area, it visits this field for a while. It is, however, but a small reminder of the glorious days of airships.

Happily, there are people today who are again planning to build huge new rigid airships, and they are considering using the same hangar. They have decided that these dirigibles are valuable in many ways, for commerce and transportation. Perhaps, one day soon, construction of a new dirigible will begin. Then, once again we may see those glorious ships of the sky sailing overhead.

Bibliography

The vast majority of illustrations in this book were derived from official U.S. Navy photographs taken between 1925 and 1935. The works presented here are secondary sources and are suggested for further reading.

Allen, Hugh, *The Story of the Airship,* Goodyear Co., Akron, OH, 1931

Beaubois, Henry, *Airships,* Two Continents Publishing, NY, 1976

Botting, Douglas, *The Giant Airships,* Time-Life, Alexandria, VA, 1982

Dallison, Ken, *When Zeppelins Flew,* Time-Life Books, NY, 1969

Dwiggins, Don, *The Complete Book of Airships,* Tab Books, Bluebridge Summit, PA, 1981

Ege, Lennart, *Balloons and Airships,* MacMillan Publishing, NY, 1974

Hook, Tom, *Shenandoah Saga,* Airshow Publishers, Annapolis, MD, 1973

Hook, Tom, *Skyship,* Airshow Publishers, Annapolis, MD, 1976

Horton, Edward, *The Age of the Airship,* Henry Regnery Co., Chicago, IL, 1973

Litchfield, P.W., *Why Has America No Rigid Airships?,* 7 C's Press, Riverside, CT, 1945

Payne, Lee, *Lighter Than Air,* A.S. Barnes & Co., Cranbury, NJ, 1977

White, William, *Airships For the Future,* Sterling Publishing, NY, 1976

Index

105